THE BEST OF

2001

'Let them eat cake'

MATTHEW PRITCHETT studied at St Martin's School of Art in London and first saw himself published in the *New Statesman* during one of its rare lapses from high seriousness. He has been *The Daily Telegraph*'s front-page pocket cartoonist since 1988. In 1995, 1996 and 1999 he was the winner of the Cartoon Arts Trust Award, in 1991 he was 'What the Papers Say' Cartoonist of the Year and in 1996, 1998 and 2000 he was *UK Press Gazette* Cartoonist of the Year.

The Daily Telegraph

THE BEST OF

2001

'WAIT!...I can make
RoboDog wave goodbye'

ORION

Orion Books
A division of the Orion Publishing Group Ltd
Orion House
5 Upper St Martin's Lane
London WC2H 9EA

First published by Orion Books in 2001

© 2001 Telegraph Group Limited

The right of Matthew Pritchett to be identified as the
author of this work has been asserted by him in accordance
with the Copyright, Designs and Patents Act, 1988

A CIP catalogue record for this book
is available from the British Library

ISBN 0 75284 428 8

Printed and bound in Great Britain by
The Guernsey Press Co. Ltd, Guernsey, C. I.

THE BEST OF

'I've either just done our
weekly shop at Tesco,
or I've adopted twins'

Law and Order

Law and Order

'How do you find the defendant – guilty or not yet guilty?'

Law and Order

'Yes, this is your husband's phone, I've just stolen it... no, I won't bring you some milk and a loaf of bread'

World of Science

World of Science

That Census

'Darling please don't leave me — I'll have to fill in the census form all over again'

'I wouldn't mention the fact that we're cattle on the census form'

The Countryside

'We're going walkies but, remember, NO HUNTING'

The Countryside

'I only had a bacon sandwich'

The Countryside

The Countryside

'Your Agriculture Minister has been worrying my sheep'

'Dry mouth, blistered feet, I'm afraid I'll have to slaughter you'

The Countryside

'And how would sir like his
steak vaccinated?'

'Sir, I think I heard on the news
that pigswill has been banned'

The Countryside

'Will you come and carve
the sausage?'

The Countryside

The Countryside

'Excuse me, we think we own a country cottage round here, but it's been such a long time…'

The General Election

The General Election

'You should be Prime Minister,
you don't like meeting
real people either'

The General Election

'If you don't abstain on June 7th
your apathy will go unheard'

'When Mr Hague starts
saying he's going to win
the next election he's
had enough to drink'

The General Election

'Drive these to the inner cities and wait for them to be stolen'

'At least there won't be a need for any messy recounts'

The General Election

'It was self-defence'

Prescott's Punch

The General Election

'*I'm on the unleaded wing of
the Conservative Party*'

The General Election

The General Election

'I believe there are still a lot of tea leaves who haven't made up their minds yet'

The General Election

The General Election

The Tory Leadership Election

'At least it's an election a Tory can win'

'Shaun Woodward is on the phone. Can he come back and be leader?'

The Tory Leadership Election

'Michael Portillo has asked us to take out Ken Clarke's phone lines'

'I hate these Conservative leadership elections'

The Tory Leadership Election

'I hope there'll be room in the new Tory party for people who aren't at ease with the modern world'

"It's turned into a vicious battle between the 'Inclusives' and the 'Uniters'"

The Railways

'One forgets that all trains
used to go as fast as this'

The Railways

'But, darling, I thought you were
coming home by train'

'I knew we should have
gone by camel'

The Railways

'I'm afraid the 8.17 has had a
near-miss with the timetable'

'The next train is the overnight
sleeper service from Clapham
Junction to Victoria'

The US Elections

'The latest figure we're getting
is that 49.5% of everything
I've said is rubbish'

'Maybe it will be my spoilt
ballot paper that will
decide the whole thing'

The US Elections

'Does that look like a vote for
Al Gore or George Bush?'

The US Elections

'If Al Gore concedes I'll sue'

Weather or not...

The Floods

The Floods

'If you think this is bad you should see Uckfield'

'I just hope this keeps John Prescott out'

The Fuel Crisis

The Fuel Crisis

'This will teach the
Government a lesson!'

The Fuel Crisis

'NO, STOP! I really have run out of petrol'

'I fell in love with you long before I knew you worked in a filling station'

The Fuel Crisis

'It's no good. I've tried four different places but nobody wants to hear my petrol queue story'

'Another glass of milk?'

Panic buying

Metric Martyr

'Sarge, I think these scales
are in pounds and ounces'

'Help . . . police . . . robbery . . .
assault . . . mugging . . .
BANANAS 25p A POUND!'

Metric Martyr

'I want you to imagine that hut is a greengrocer's selling vegetables in pounds and ounces'

'My tax demand has been twinned with one in France'

The Modern Military

'The gays aren't
going to like this'

'You're going to meet a tall,
dark, handsome stranger
and shoot him'

The Modern Military

'My goodness, Lance Bombardier,
you're beautiful without your
night vision binoculars'

'It's B Company, sir,
I'm afraid it's eloped'

Foreign Affairs

'I need a packed lunch. Our French teacher is taking us to blockade a petrol station'

Foreign Affairs

'Oh no, I'm wearing the same
outfit I wore to watch
last year's Oscars'

'You've been looking
a lot smarter since Nicole
Kidman became single'

Foreign Affairs

'I really am too ill to work, when I was spotted in the pub last night, that was library footage'

The Slump

'I wish you wouldn't bring your work home'

'Things got so bad we had to call in the army'

Sleaze

'I think I may have been
rushed into confessing
something I didn't do'

Sleaze

'Days when Mr Mandelson doesn't resign seem so flat'

'Yes, I think this government is sleazy, but a tenner could persuade me to change my mind'

The Health Service

'Try throwing money at me'

'Darling, introduce yourself to
that miserable looking man, he
must be a doctor'

I'm your pilot and I'm drunk

'One more for the runway?'

'Ladies and gentlemen, either
we're experiencing some
turbulence or I have the
mother of all hangovers'

A multi-cultural society

And finally...

'Maybe modern artists would leave London if people stopped feeding them'

'Before you say no, let me outline some of the tax benefits...'

And finally…

And finally...

'I'm sick of running from MAFF. I want to come home and give myself up'

And finally…

Sophie Wessex tricked

'Come inside, you're attracting the vulture'

And Finally . . .

'We beat the West Indies in 1969
and AGAIN this year — it's
getting to be monotonous'

'We interrupt this programme
to tell you what time
News at Ten will be on'

And Finally . . .

And Finally . . .

'We call him The Dome;
he's very expensive and
we can't get rid of him'

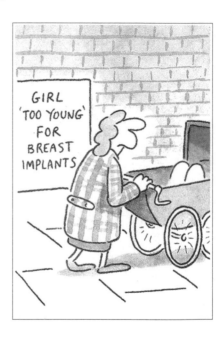

And Finally . . .

'He tried to switch off the
final episode of Morse'

And Finally . . .

'We want an area with
good schools and an
active local lynch mob'

Vigilantes hound
paedophiles

'We'll allow the homophobia and
misogyny but while you're in
Britain don't mention the euro'

And Finally . . .

And Finally . . .

'I'm afraid the stork that
delivered you flew off
with your £500'

'Release the hostages, give up
your guns and tell us what
you've had from the minibar'

Kidnappers hold
holidaymakers

And Finally . . .

And Finally . . .

'I met a wonderful man at the airport, but we only had 52 all-too-brief hours together'

'3.7% is excellent, sir, I nearly got that in a maths exam'

And Finally . . .

'We've just voted you out of the house'

And Finally . . .

'I'm a millionaire on paper...
but it's a very old bit of paper'

'Is it insensitive to have the
anti-capitalism riot during a
global economic downturn?'

And Finally . . .

Speeding fine for
Princess Anne

And Finally . . .

'STREWTH! This must be what it feels like to be a Pom'

'I'm going to explain Public, Private Partnerships until you feel drowsy and fall asleep'

And Finally . . .

'Just think how much later
they'd be if they stopped
at every red light'

And Finally . . .

'I'm just popping out to Lambeth,
I'll need some cannabis for
Henman's match today'

And Finally . . .

'We want to claim the £3m jackpot but we seem to have accidentally picked the wrong numbers'

And Finally . . .

'YOU'RE FRIED!'

'Maybe it's all these late night sittings, but I think I'm falling in love with you'